CHILDREN AT THE HEARTH

by
Barbara Swell

Order No. NGB-820   ISBN 1-883206-34-0

INTRODUCTION

Kids are kids; always have been. If you take two modern-day 9 year olds and plunk them in a rocky creek next to a tall pine forest on a breezy Spring afternoon, they'll do the same thing two 9 year olds from 1858 would have done. They'll take off their shoes and wade in the cold water, looking under rocks for crawdads. When their feet have turned to ice, they'll warm up in the sun with a mud pie picnic.

Of course, the 1858 kids probably didn't have any shoes to begin with. They played in the creek after milking cows, feeding chickens, collecting eggs, and walking 5 miles to and from school. And even though life is easier (yet more complicated) for families in the second Millennium, if you pry the electronic screens away from today's kids, you'll find they're still interested in the timeless ponderings of childhood. Like what happens if you hold lizzard eggs in your hands, and how to prevent ugliness.

This book is an invitation to learn about the lives of children past at the kitchen table of today. Why in the kitchen, you ask? Because for as long as people can remember, the pulse of family life beat hardest where kinship and stories of the day's adventures blended over a pan of chicken and dumplings.

Have fun cooking and sharing stories of the past and present with the children at your hearth!

Eating for Wealth

- *Eat cabbage on New Year's day to have money all year.*
- *You'll have the same amount of dollars as the number of peas you eat on New Year's day.*[6]

TABLE OF CONTENTS

SAFETY

Cooking is a high risk activity for a kid. Have you ever seen someone with singed (burnt) eyebrows? It's not a pretty sight. Please follow the instructions below:

• Have an adult supervise you at all stages of cooking.

• Wash your hands.

• Tie back long hair and roll up your sleeves.

• Use hot pads to handle hot pans. A damp or wet hot pad is like using your bare hands to take a pan out of the oven.

• When opening the oven door, stand back first or you'll soon smell burnt eyebrows.

• When cooking in a pan on the stove, turn handles toward the back of the stove so you don't accidently bump into the hot pan.

• Don't even think about frying anything without an adult around; mistakes could be very serious.

• Treat raw meat as though it is poisonous (bacteria found on it can make you extremely sick). Cut raw meat on a plate, never a wooden chopping block, and wash your hands with hot soapy water after handling.

• When using a knife, keep fingers on top of the knife and cut away from you or down onto your chopping board. See the girl to the left? She's cutting bread the wrong way, toward herself. She could easily get cut!

• **Clean up your mess!!!**

How-To's

Cooking takes practice; think of it as an edible art form. Some dishes will turn out great, and some will end up in the compost pile. If you have a relative who loves to cook, be sure to ask them to teach you what they know. I'll bet you get to hear stories and some good advice, too. Above all, have fun.

MEASURING

19th century cooks did not measure foods for cooking the way we do today. They used teacups, their hands, and their eyeballs. An example of eyeball measuring is "add a lump of butter the size of an egg." Some of the recipes in this book call for old-timey measuring creativity, but most use modern measures.

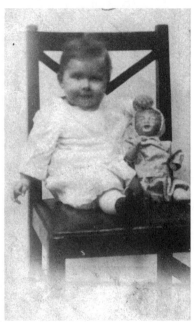

You'll probably be using things like mixers, food processors, and ice to make these foods which were not available before the 1900's. Did you know how folks got ice back then? They collected it in blocks from frozen ponds and buried it in sawdust underground 'til summer!

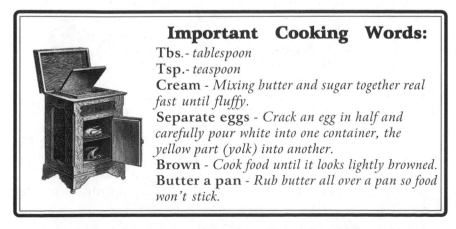

Important Cooking Words:

Tbs.- *tablespoon*

Tsp.- *teaspoon*

Cream - *Mixing butter and sugar together real fast until fluffy.*

Separate eggs - *Crack an egg in half and carefully pour white into one container, the yellow part (yolk) into another.*

Brown - *Cook food until it looks lightly browned.*

Butter a pan - *Rub butter all over a pan so food won't stick.*

PLANNING YOUR MEAL

There's not really much to planning a good meal. Remember that the cook gets to make what he feels like eating! Most kids don't shop for food, so you have two choices for meal planning, depending on your personality:

1. The spontaneous, **fly-by-the-seat-of-the-pants cook** will look in the cabinet and refrigerator and throw things together that seem like they'd be good. What seems good depends on your mood. You know who you are...you're the one who's always mixing up concoctions at the counter that bubble, fizz, and ooze. You don't want a recipe or anyone else to tell you what to do. You don't need a shopper.

2. If you're a **plan-ahead cook,** you will decide in advance what you want to prepare, and then give the shopper a list of ingredients to buy. You like to follow recipes.

Photo courtesy David C. Anderson

What to Cook:
Good cooks use this formula for each meal:
a protein + a vegetable or fruit + a starch
You know what a vegetable and a fruit is; a protein is meat, milk, beans, or cheese. A starch is usually something like potatoes, grains, or noodles. You can mix everything up and call it a casserole, but kids don't usually like that. Be sure your meal includes a variety of colors and textures.

SETTING THE TABLE

I f you were an 1850's pioneer child living in a sod house, setting the table would be easy. Each person had one hand carved wooden spoon, and there would be a wooden plate (called a trencher) for each adult. Two or more kids would share one plate. Some families brought china dishes with them on their journey West, but if the dishes made it without breaking, kids didn't get to use them.

I know you already know how to set a table...but you only do it when someone reminds you about 80 times, right? But did you know that setting the table is one of the most important jobs in the house? The families that sit down together at least once a day for a meal are the happiest. And when your family sits down to a table set with care and artistic flare, they'll thank you for it!

A Bad Meal

A bad meal (one my husband really cooked):
Potatoes, rice, oatmeal, and bread

A good meal (like I make):
Chicken pot pie with green beans and fruit salad

MANNERS

A child's place in the family and community was very different in early America than it is today. If you lived here in the 1600's, you were expected to obey your parents. If you didn't, the consequences were harsh. You could be taken away from your parents, or even be killed as a result of this law:

THE STUBBORN CHILD LAW

This Massachusetts law was passed in 1646 because citizens thought children were getting too wild and unruly. Ask an adult to explain it to you.

"If a man has a stubborn or rebellious son, of sufficient years and understanding (16 years of age), which will not obey the voice of his Father or the voice of his Mother, and that when they have chastened him will not hearken unto them: then shall his Father and Mother being his natural parents, lay hold on him, and bring him to the Magistrates assembled in Court and testify unto them, that their son is stubborn and rebellious and will not obey their voice and chastisement, but lives in sundry notorious crimes, such a son shall be put to death."

Fortunately, no children were ever actually killed under this law (which of course, no longer exists), but I'll bet they obeyed their parents more as a result of it!

MANNERS

I f you were from a wealthy family in the 19th century, you were cared for by a nurse in a separate wing of the house. "Nurse" fed you, disciplined you, played with you, and took care of you when you were sick. She took you to visit your parents occasionally, and when you saw them, you had to be dressed well and on your best behavior.

Pioneer and farm children were much more a part of their families than were the children of the rich. Their help was needed because there was so much work to be done. These children spent time with their families, but they clearly had their place.

When meal time came, parents ate first, kids ate last, often standing and sharing plates with their siblings. The best piece of meat went to the father. And children didn't complain. They ate what they were served; they were HUNGRY!

THE GOOPS

The goops, they lick their fingers,
The goops they lick their knives,
And they spill their broth on the tablecloth
Oh, they lead disgusting lives!

The goops, they talk while eating,
And loud and fast they chew,
And that is why I'm glad that I-
Am not a goop.....are you?
                    by Gelett Burgess

MANNERS

HOW TO BEHAVE, 1800's

• Be kind and gentle in your manners.

• Do not become peevish and pout because you do not get everything you want. Be satisfied with what is given to you.

• Do always as your parents bid you. Obey them with a ready mind and a pleasant face.
McGuffey's 3rd Reader

• Next to goodness, strive to obtain knowledge. Never forget that by practice and perserverance, *you can learn anything.*

• Have a scrupulous regard to neatness of person. Broken strings and tangled hair are signs that little girls are not very industrious in any of their habits.

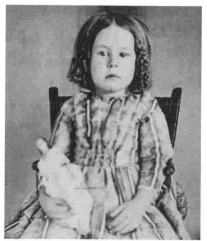

Photo courtesy Library of Congress

• Cherish love for your brothers and sisters. Let your words and actions be such toward them, as you wish they had been, should death separate you from each other. (Children died all too often from diseases and infections when this was written).
-*The Girls Own Book, 1834*

> *Green eye, greedy gut,*
> *Steal a pig and eat it up;*
> *Brown eye, pickety pie;*
> *Run around and tell a lie!*

MANNERS

19TH CENTURY SHAKER ADVICE TO CHILDREN ON BEHAVIOR AT THE TABLE

Cut your meat both neat and square,
And take of both an equal share.
Also, of bones you'll take your due,
For bones and meat together grew.

Don't pick your teeth, or ears, or nose,
Nor scratch your head, nor tonk your toes;
Nor belch nor sniff, nor jest nor pun,
Nor have the least of play or fun.

Photo by Gideon Laney, courtesy of David C. Anderson

Weird & Disgusting Foods

N o early American cookbook would be complete without including some recipes for foods no modern kid would eat. Here is a smattering of things you might have found on your plate 100 years ago. And remember, no pickled tongue...no dessert!

1832 Pickled, Glazed Tongue

"Boil a large tongue till it be tender, skin and glaze it, and serve it with mashed turnips on one side, and mashed carrots, or carrots and spinach on the other."[25]

Photo courtesy University of Louisville photographic archives, KY

1832 Stewed Eels With Anchovies

"Cut eels into pieces, season well with salt and pepper; then add butter, sorrel, sage, onion, lemon peel and chopped anchovy. Pour a pint of water over the top and stew for half an hour. Serve with nutmeg, and the juice of half a lemon."[25]

Weird & Disgusting Foods

Fred stands on top of a bee-gum (bee hive) in the Tennessee mountains in the early 1900's.

Chocolate Sandwiches

1 large banana
2 Tbs. cocoa

Mash banana to a cream, then add the cocoa. Stir in about 3 tablespoons of mayonnaise and spread between buttered slices of bread.[24]

New Sandwiches

Add 2 tablespons water to 3 tablespons of peanut butter. Beat until creamy and add 2 tablespons of catsup. Mix well and spread on unbuttered bread.[24]

Boys in Dresses

Can you guess why the boys in these pictures are wearing dresses? In generations past, infant and toddler boys wore dresses up until the time they were toilet-trained. They had no plastic pants to put over their diapers to keep their clothes dry, and people didn't wash clothes or bodies very often.

BEVERAGES

City dwellers with money had their choice of beverages in the 1850's. Pineapples and lemons were carried from the southern regions of our country and South America by boat and train to those living in cities and towns on the east coast and the Midwest. The poor drank milk (if they had a cow), or water that was often full of germs from polluted wells and rivers.

Settler children drank milk, water, and even coffee, beer, and other fermented beverages. Pioneer children who missed drinking lemonade were given water mixed with vinegar and molasses as a substitute.

STRAWBERRY WATER

1 cup strawberries with caps removed
½ cup sugar
4 cups cold water
Juice of one lemon

Crush the strawberries with the back of a wooden spoon. Add one cup of the water and rub mixture through a screened tea strainer, (or you could whirl them in the blender). Add the sugar, lemon juice and remaining three cups of water. Serve over ice with a lemon slice placed on the edge of the cup.

Drinking Shoe Leather

It was once thought that adding milk to tea created a substance related to leather. That's why people would say, "People who put milk in tea are drinking boots and shoes in disguise."[23]

Bad Hair Day?

Maybe, but children and adults often wore hairpieces (small wigs) attached to their own hair in the 1890's when this photo was taken.

BEVERAGES

Settler families were large. In this picture, a woman and her mother are photographed with ten children on the front porch of their Appalachian mountain cabin.

PINEAPPLE-ADE

Peel a fresh, very ripe pineapple and cut it up into very small pieces. Sprinkle some sugar on top, then smash with a potato masher or a cup. Add water (you decide how much) and pour into a pitcher with a strainer lid. Chill for a few hours, then pour over ice.

LEMONADE

Squeeze the juice from 3 lemons, mix with 2 cups water and add sugar to taste. (Maybe you should get a second opinion from an adult about what "to taste" means.)

MILK PUNCH

Add one tablespoon of sugar to a cup of milk. Heat it, but don't boil and sprinkle nutmeg or cinnamon on top.

BEVERAGES

MAKE-DO HOT COCOA

Warm up a cup of milk, but don't let it boil. Add a tablespoon of sugar and whatever chocolate you can find. You can use 1 tablespoon of cocoa powder, a handful of chocolate chips, or half a chocolate candy bar. Stir until the chocolate melts, and add a couple drops of real vanilla extract. Serve as is or topped with whipped cream.

HOT MULLED CIDER

1 quart apple cider
1 Tbs. brown sugar

1 cinnamon stick
½ lemon, sliced

Combine all the ingredients in a saucepan. Heat on low for about 15 minutes or long enough for the delicious smell to waft through your house.

Photo courtesy Great Smoky Mt. National Park

A playhouse, built by four Tennessee mountain boys under the age of 12 yrs.

GHOSTS

G host stories are as much a part of childhood as candy eating and crawdad hunting. Why, kids scared themselves silly with "haint" tales in the 1800's just as much as they do today. Here's an interesting and true story that comes out of the hills of rural Greenbrier County, West Virginia.

THE GREENBRIER GHOST

In 1897, a dapper man named Edward Shue of Rainelle, West Virginia married a pretty 15 year old girl named Zona Heaster. Edward was not known for being nice to his three former wives (two of whom died sudden, violent deaths); however, he seemed to love his new bride, Zona. But about two months after they married, she was found dead as well. A physician said it was probably heart failure that killed her.

Well, Zona's mother, Mrs. Heaster, was heartbroken, as you can imagine. About a week after the funeral, Zona appeared to her on four different nights telling her mother that Edward got mad and killed her by breaking her neck. Mrs. Heaster took that information to the local sheriff. They dug Zona up, and verified that, indeed, her neck had been broken.

When the case went to court, Edward Shue was convicted by a jury of murdering his wife, Zona. This is the only documented court case in our country where a man was proven guilty using the testimony of a ghost. And if you go to Route 60 in Greenbrier County, West Virginia, you'll see a historical marker that tells the true story of *The Greenbrier Ghost*!

Real Words Written on a Nevada Gravestone	*Here lays Butch,* *We planted him raw.* *He was quick on the trigger,* *But slow on the draw.*

Soups & Stews

Just about every child has dreamed of leaving home like a hobo in search of a life with no grown-ups to boss them around. Maybe when your parents were little, they wrapped some meager belongings in a bandana, tied the bundle to a long stick, and wandered about the back yard in search of a train that would carry them to freedom.

The heyday of the American hobo arrived after the Civil War when trains (the preferred mode of hobo transportation) crisscrossed the country. The hobo was most often a bright and talented man with a restless soul who wandered from town to town, riding the rails in search of skilled work.

Armed with a trusty pocket knife, the hobo whittled in his spare time, trading carvings for food or selling them for a little money. When the hobo got hungry, he made camp and threw whatever food he had into a pot and made a stew of it. Next time you and your hobo buddies go camping, try making this stew:

Hobo Mulligan Stew

5 potatoes, cubed   3 carrots, peeled & chunked
1 onion, chopped   2 cups water
1 lb. lean meat (beef, lamb, chicken, or pork)

Cut the meat into 1 inch cubes and brown in a little butter in a frying pan. In a saucepan, add the meat, potatoes, carrots, and

onions. Pour the water in and simmer on low heat for at least one hour. Check the liquid level as it's cooking, and add more water if needed. Sprinkle in salt and pepper to taste. If you have fresh or dried thyme, add a little after 30 minutes of cooking. Serves 4-6.

Soups & Stews

Photo courtesy So.Appalachian Photographic Archive, Mars Hill College, N.C.

Tomato Bisque

1 can whole tomatoes
1 cup whole milk
Pepper to taste

1 tsp. sugar
½ onion, chopped
Green herbs

Cook onion in a teaspoon of oil until soft. Add sugar, tomatoes and juice. Simmer on low heat about 30 minutes. When the tomatoes have turned into little pieces, add the milk. Cook 5 minutes on low heat. DO NOT LET THE SOUP BOIL after adding milk, or it will curdle. Season with fresh or dried herbs; basil or thyme are good. Serve this soup with grated cheddar cheese sprinkled on top. Grilled cheese sandwiches or cheese biscuits go mighty good with tomato soup. Serves 4-6.

SOUPS & STEWS

PEANUT SOUP

1 onion, chopped
1 stalk celery, chopped
1 tsp. butter

2 cans chicken broth
1 cup milk
1 cup peanut butter

Cook onion and celery in butter until soft. Add chicken broth and cook 5 minutes. This is a creamy soup, so you can either strain out the onions and celery, or blend them in the food processor with a little water until they're almost liquid. Add the milk and peanut butter and heat, but don't boil. This soup is rich (which means it fills you up fast), so serve it in little bowls with chopped peanuts on top. Serves 6.

To Get Your Wish

• *Spit on a bridge, then go away.*
• *Kiss the hem of your skirt if it turns up.*
• *Make a wish when you try on another person's shoe.*
• *If you see a white horse, stamp it. To stamp, lick your right index finger and touch it to your left palm. Then lightly hit the place you touched with a right-handed fist.*

CREAMY CORN SOUP

1 can creamed corn
1 onion, chopped
Pepper and salt to taste

2 cups whole milk
Popcorn

Cook the chopped onion in a little dab of butter until soft. Add the corn and the milk. Heat at a very low temperature for 5 minutes, but do not boil. If you want to be authentic, use corn that is freshly grated off the cob and add the cob scrapings to the soup. Three ears of corn will substitute for one can. Serve the soup with a bowl of popcorn that your guests can sprinkle on top right before eating (popcorn gets soggy real fast). Serves 4.

SOUPS & STEWS

CHICKEN SOUP & HOMEMADE NOODLES

You may think this soup is too much work, but I'm leaving out the hard part...which is, go out and kill a chicken, gut it, then dip it in boiling water and pluck its feathers out! Have an adult prepare the soup while you make the noodles. This serves 4-6.

Soup:

½ chicken, cut into pieces	2 stalks celery, sliced
1 quart water	2 carrots, sliced
1 onion, diced	Parsley, bay leaf, garlic

Combine chicken, onion, celery, 1 carrot, and water. Throw in a bit of fresh parsley, 1 bay leaf, and a sliced clove or two of garlic. Simmer this for 1-2 hours, or cook in a crockpot all day. Let the mixture cool 20 minutes, then strain the broth and take the chicken off the bones. Add the chicken and the other sliced carrot back to the strained broth. Just before time to eat, season the soup with salt and pepper, bringing it to a boil. Add the cooked noodles to the soup and simmer about 3 minutes more.

Noodles:

    1 cup flour
    ½ tsp. salt
    1 Tbs. butter

Rub these together real well, add an egg, and 1 or 2 Tbs. water. Stir until the mixture forms a ball, then roll out on a floured board as thin as you can get it. Cut into strips, and cook 3 minutes in boiling water. Your noodles will look "rustic", that is, not store-bought. That is a good thing. Tell your guests that you meant to make old-timey chicken and dough-blob soup.

Photo by William Barnhill courtesy Mars Hill College, N.C.

PIONEERS

Gold! The cry was heard around the world after nuggets of gold were discovered in California in the Spring of 1848. Lured by the promise of instant wealth, 300,000 pioneers traveled the Oregon Trail through 2,000 miles of desolate plains and rugged mountains headed for the West Coast. The trail was littered with household furniture and precious belongings that had to be discarded to lighten the load for tired oxen pulling heavy wagons. Hungry travelers ate boring food on the journey,...mostly hard tack, dried beef, bacon, and cornmeal mush.

Another wave of pioneers settled the midwestern plains from the 1860's through the 1890's. These homesteaders built sod houses made from blocks of grass and dirt because there were no trees. They burned "cow pies" for fuel! Settlers hunted buffalo for food, sport, and clothing until they were all but extinct, forcing Plains Indians from their homeland.

Trains crossed the country by 1869, making travel easier, and food more accessible. Now pioneers could buy oranges from Florida and dishes from England (if they had the money).

The Chrisman Sisters, 1886   Photo courtesy Nebraska State Historical Society

These sisters have claimed their land from the government and built a sod house to live in. Sometimes snakes found their way inside the "soddies", but the dirt houses kept the rain out and the heat in during the cold winter months.

BREAD

HARD TACK, 1836

Hard Tack is a HARD cracker that keeps well for great periods of time and doesn't weigh much...perfect for a long journey. For countless generations, these crackers have kept many a pioneer and soldier from starving.

2 cups white flour
Pinch salt

1 Tbs. butter
Milk

Rub butter and salt into flour, and add enough milk to make a stiff dough. Knead the dough 15 minutes. Roll out ½ inch thick and cut with a small teacup. Prick with a fork, bake about 300° until lightly browned. Hang to dry (in a burlap sack), then store in a cool, dry place for your journey.

HARD TACK YOU CAN EAT

These crackers break too easily to tote around for long, but at least you can eat them without losing a tooth, and they're good.

2 cups self-rising flour
½ stick butter
½ cup water or milk

Rub butter into the flour. Add enough water or milk to make a stiff dough. Knead it a minute on a floured board, then roll out about ¼ inch thick. Cut into squares with a knife, then prick the top of each cracker with a fork two times. Put on a greased cookie sheet and bake at 300° until lightly browned.

BREAD

CORN EGG BREAD, 1881

This recipe comes from a great book called "What Mrs. Fisher Knows About Old Southern Cooking." She had been a slave and was not allowed to learn to read or write. So she dictated her recipes to a group of women, who then published this book. Mrs. Abby Fisher was the first African American woman to write and publish a cookbook! You can make the recipe below, but remember to melt the butter in an iron skillet, then pour the batter back into the skillet, and bake in a 400° oven for 25 minutes.

"Two well-beaten eggs, one pint of meal, half pint of sour milk, one teaspoonful of soda, one tablespoon melted butter. Mix all together, stir well. Bake in an ordinary pan."[11]

Courtesy of the Library of Congress

Photo by Matthew Brady

The Real Tom Thumb

Charles Stratton was born in 1838 in New York. He had Pituitary Dwarfism and only grew to be about 28 inches tall. P.T. Barnum (the circus man) discovered Charlie at age five and invited him to perform at his show on Broadway under the name of General Tom Thumb. Barnum taught the bright 2 foot tall, 15 pound child to do skits, tell jokes, and dance. His popular shows in America and Europe earned Charlie $250 a day and more for many years. He married a woman, also a little person, in 1863, and together they lived the fancy life. They traveled in a miniature carriage, and owned a mansion, a yacht, and lots of horses. Charlie died at age 45 in 1883. In this glass photo, he's about 20 years old.

BREAD

CAT HEAD BISCUITS

When most people think of biscuits, little round flaky breads come to mind. Not so here in the South. When Yankees see our biscuits, they say, "Why that thing's biggern' a cat head!" I won't even mention the grits and sawmill gravy that you're supposed to eat with them.

2 cups flour	1 tsp. salt
2 tsp. baking powder	Milk
¼ cup butter or solid vegetable shortening	

Combine dry ingredients, then rub the butter in until no lumps are visible. Add enough milk to make a soft dough that you can handle. Knead a minute on a floured board. Here's the cat head part...pinch off pieces of the dough about half as big as you think the finished biscuit should be. Now slightly flatten it with your hands. Place on a buttered cookie sheet and bake in a hot 400° preheated oven to cook about 10-15 minutes until lightly browned. Serve at once.

CHEESE CRESCENTS

Make biscuit dough above and divide into two balls. Roll each ball out thin into a circle and sprinkle grated cheddar cheese on top. Cut each circle like a pie into eight pieces. Roll up starting at the big end, then bake as above. For **cinnamon crescents**, brush the circles with melted butter, then sprinkle cinnamon sugar on top before slicing and rolling.

CHILDREN IN SLAVERY

Not all early 19th century African Americans were bound by slavery, but for most of those who were, everyday life was a challenge. The majority lived on Southern plantations where they were given a small cabin to live in, minimal clothing, medical care, and a ration of food for their family. Most enslaved African Americans grew a kitchen garden (small vegetable garden) to supplement the cornmeal, bacon, pork, and potatoes that they received from their "master." If the plantation was large, the slave families would prepare community meals and the children who were too young to work in the fields helped out with the cooking.

These next three pages include games children in slavery played and recipes for typical cornmeal breads they would have eaten. For an interesting account of actual stories from former slave children, children 9 years and older may want to read selected pages in the books edited by Belenda Hermence, referenced on page 69.

Games of Children in Slavery

Most slave children weren't required to work until they were about 11 years old. They often played with the children from the "big house" in smaller plantations. The games they played were the same that all kids played during that period of time with two exceptions:

1. *Enslaved children didn't play with "bought" toys, except maybe a ball. Their families were given no money.*

2. *They didn't play games where someone was left out or eliminated. Knowing that you or a family member could be sold to another plantation owner, these children didn't want this fear to enter the world of their play.*[19]

CHILDREN IN SLAVERY

Photo courtesy Library of Congress

This photograph from the 1860's was called "Five Generations on Smith's Plantation." Since slaves were considered property, they were not allowed to marry legally. Of course, they married anyway, but secretly. The family in this picture managed to keep themselves together at a time when African American families were often separated.

House Ball

The two-room houses built for slave families were small enough to easily throw a ball over. For this game, a large group of children would split off into two groups, half on one side of the house, half on the other. The first group would throw a ball over the roof to the other group. Whoever caught the ball would run over to the other side of the house and tag one of the other players with the ball. Then everybody would go back to their places.[14]

BREAD

CORN DODGERS, 1850

Mix self-rising cornmeal with a little melted butter and enough water to form a soft dough you can handle. Form into patties and place on a greased skillet. Cook in a hot 400° oven until browned.

ASH CAKE

Build a fire in your hearth, then clear the coals from a spot. Put your Corn Dodger on that clean space and let it cook. When a crust forms on the top, cover it with hot ashes to finish baking. Brush off the ashes before eating.

*Note: *If you want to try this, put the cornmeal patty onto a piece of buttered foil in the hearth and cover it with more foil before putting the hot ashes on top.*

HOE CAKE

Put your Corn Dodger on top of a clean, buttered hoe blade. Bake over coals in your fireplace. When the bottom's brown, flip it.

Photo courtesy Library of Congress

A young 37 yr. old Abe Lincoln poses for famous early photographer, Matthew Brady, long before the Civil War.

Roley Hole

This game is for two or more people. Ask your parents if you can dig a hole in the ground just big enough to hold a tennis ball. Put the tennis ball some distance away from the hole. The player who kicks the ball into the hole scores a point. You make up the rest of the rules![15]

BREAD

SOFT PRETZELS

Pretzels can be made from any Italian bread recipe. Beginners may want to use frozen bread dough until you get the hang of twisting the dough into pretzel shapes. If you're using fresh dough, let it rise until doubled before beginning the recipe below.

Take a piece of dough the size of a golf ball and cover it with flour. Roll it out like a snake about 12 inches long. Now, using this picture as a guide, shape your pretzel. Be sure to pinch the two ends

down well so your pretzel holds together when you bake it. Carefully, lay it onto a greased cookie sheet. Brush each pretzel with melted butter and lightly sprinkle with kosher or coarse salt. Let rise 15 minutes and bake in a preheated 400° oven for 15 minutes or until lightly browned.

PEASANT CASSEROLE BREAD

This is a good yeast bread that's easy enough for beginning bakers. No kneading is required.

1 pkg. yeast	1 cup warm water
1½ tsp. salt	4 cups bread flour
1 Tbs. sugar	

Dissolve the yeast in warm (**not** hot) water. Add the sugar and salt, stirring well. Combine the liquid and three cups of the flour. Stir until you have a soft, wet dough that holds together. Add more of the flour, if needed. Put the ball of dough in a large buttered bowl to rise until doubled in size (about 1 hour). Punch down and put in a buttered casserole dish. Let it rise again until doubled and bake in a preheated 375° oven 40 minutes until browned.

MEAT

D o you know what it means to eat everything on a pig except the squeal? In generations past, people didn't waste a bite of meat, for it was hard to get and time consuming to prepare. The recipes in this section make use of small pieces of meat mixed with other foods so you can know what it's like to stretch what you have as far as possible to feed your family of ten. Aren't you glad I left out the recipe for chicken foot stew?

Photo courtesy Fred Hultstrand History in Pictures, NDIRS-NDSU, Fargo

PIONEER SAUSAGE AND APPLES

1 package sausage links
5 Tbs. brown sugar or real maple syrup
8 tart apples, sliced

Have an adult cook the sausage, drain on paper towels, and pour off the fat. Cut the cooked sausages up and put back into the frying pan with the sliced apples. Cook until the apples are tender, then add sugar or syrup and cook on low heat a few minutes. Serves 6.

MEAT

KABOBS

An adult will need to prepare this, but kids will like to eat it. Cut lean (that means not much fat) pork, chicken, or beef into cubes. Put on bamboo skewers along with onions and squash cubes, or forget the vegetables if you don't like them. Soak the kabobs in Italian (not fat free) dressing for at least an hour before cooking on the grill. Take the swords, I mean skewers, out of the kabobs before serving to kids.

MEAT HASH

Dice (cut real small) one potato per person. Cut up whatever cooked leftover meat you have on hand into real small pieces. Put a teaspoon of butter in a skillet and cook the potatoes until almost tender, turning often with a spatula to keep from sticking. Add the meat and maybe a chopped onion if you like. Cook hash until brown, adding a bit more butter if it sticks to the pan. Add salt and pepper to taste. A fried egg goes good with hash. Cook it in the pan after you dish out the hash or just poke a hole down in the hash and let it cook in the pan.

*Note: Hash is great on a camp-out. After dinner, bury some foiled-wrapped potatoes in the coals of the fire and cook until tender. Next morning, cut them up and add some cooked and drained sausage or other meat. Brown in a non-stick pan, then poke holes in the hash and crack an egg into each hole to cook.

Boarding Houses

Boarding Houses and the Working Class

Times were hard in Europe in the mid 1800's. Hungry and discouraged people from Ireland, England, Germany, and Scandanavia thought they could find a better life in America, the "Land of Plenty." Millions came over each year by

boat, mostly to New York. These immigrants lived in cities in hopes of finding work so they could make enough money to send for their loved ones. Men found jobs in factories and lived in crowded boarding houses with as many as 15 fellows in one room! Here's a funny song by an unknown author about bad boarding house food:

The All Go Hungry Hash House

I'm a boarder and I dwell in that second-class hotel,
If I stay here long, I think I'll go insane,
For I lay here on my bunk and I cannot reach my trunk,
And the board I owe would break a millionaire.

Oh they feed us chicken pie, if you eat it you will die,
The meat you cannot cut it with a sword,
Oh, the undertakers hang around, for there's work to be found,
In that all-go-hungry hash house where I board.

Oh, they carried me upstairs one night, I had neither gun nor knife,
It was something they had never done before,
Oh, the fleas all held me down, while the cinch bugs scrapped around
In that all-go-hungry hash house where I board.

Oh the beef-steak it was rare, and the butter had red hair,
And the baby had his feet both in the stew;
Oh, the eggs I would not touch, if you bit one it would hatch,
In that all-go-hungry hash house where I board.

MEAT

This Italian immigrant family is entering America through Ellis Island in New York. Maybe they're going to be reunited with their working father who has a room for them in a boarding house.

1892 Daily Menu for the Working Class

Breakfast - *Bread, cheese, onions, herring*
Lunch - *Bread and soup*
Dinner - *Bread and a bit of boiled meat*

MEAT

Photo Courtesy Fred Hulstrand History in Pictures Collection, NDIRS-NDSU, Fargo, ND

The woman on the right is carding wool to clean it and straighten the fibers so the woman on the left can spin it. Spinning twists the wool fibers together and creates long strands of yarn that can be knitted or woven into clothing, rugs, or coverlets.

PARMESAN CHICKEN

6 boneless chicken breasts
3 Tbs. butter
¼ cup Parmesan cheese
½ cup fine bread crumbs

Melt butter in a glass baking dish. Combine breadcrumbs and Parmesan cheese in a bowl. Dip chicken in the butter, then cover with the crumb/cheese mixture. Roll up each piece and put back in the baking dish. Cover with foil and bake at 350° for about 30 minutes. Uncover and cook another 20-30 minutes until browned.

MEAT

SUNDAY CHICKEN AND DUMPLINGS, 1863

1 fat hen, cut into pieces	2 cups milk
3 stalks celery, chopped	1 onion, chopped
Double recipe for noodle dough (pg. 21)	

Put the hen in a large pan and add enough water to just cover. Add onions and celery and simmer on low heat for 2 hours. Make sure the water does not boil out of it. After the mixture cools down a little, remove the bones from the meat and strain the broth. Put the chicken back into the broth and return to the stove. Add the milk and bring back to a simmer (a little boil). Now make your dumplings.

Dumplings:
Dumplings look like big noodles in the South, biscuits elsewhere. For noodle dumplings, double the noodle recipe on page 21, but roll out thicker, longer, and wider. For biscuit dumplings, make a recipe for biscuits, but don't roll out and cut.

For biscuit dumplings, drop batter by spoonful on top of simmering chicken. Cook covered 10 minutes, then take lid off and cook another 10 minutes. For noodle dumplings, add dough strips to simmering chicken a few at a time, stirring so they don't stick together. Cook for 20 minutes or until dumplings are done. Occasionally stir mixture so noodles don't stick to the bottom of the pan. Call in your family and serve immediately!

Sunday Pioneer Dinner

Chicken and dumplings
Wheat biscuits and butter
Corn, sweet potatoes, green beans
Buttermilk, coffee
Vinegar pie

Vegetables

Photo courtesy Denver Public Library

WINTER SQUASH WITH APPLES

1 Tbs. butter	5 Tbs. brown sugar

1 large butternut squash, peeled and diced
4 tart, firm apples, peeled and sliced

Preheat oven to 350°. Put the butter in a baking dish and melt it in the oven. Add squash and sugar, and toss to coat with butter. Cover with a lid or foil and bake for one hour. Sprinkle with cinnamon sugar before serving.

VEGETABLES

SWEET POTATO COBBLER

One sweet potato per person
One recipe biscuit dough (pg. 25), cut in thin strips
Brown sugar
Butter

Peel sweet potatoes and boil whole until tender. When they're cool, slice about 1 inch thick. Butter a baking dish and spread out a layer of potatoes. Cover with thin biscuit strips, and sprinkle with brown sugar. Repeat with another layer of potatoes, dough, and top with brown sugar or cinnamon sugar. Cover with foil or a lid and bake at 350° for about 30 minutes, until inside layer of biscuits is cooked. Take cover off and let top biscuits brown before serving. Cook this in a cast iron dutch oven if you have one.

ASH POTATOES

Wood stoves weren't available to families until the late 1860's. Cooking happened in the hearth until then. Potatoes were a popular vegetable because they were easy to grow and stored well in a cool cellar all year. They baked easily in a pile of ashes or propped up against the inside edge of the hearth. Bury foil wrapped sweet or white potatoes inside a pile of ashes in your wood stove or fireplace and see how good they taste. They take about an hour to cook, depending on the size.

VEGETABLES

SUCCOTASH

1 cup fresh or frozen lima beans
1 cup fresh, frozen or canned corn
Butter, salt, pepper, cream

Cook the beans until tender (about 20 minutes), add corn and simmer five minutes. Drain the liquid and add a little piece of butter, salt, pepper, and about 2 tablespoons of cream or milk. Pioneers would have added chopped salt pork or left-over meat.

Photo courtesy of Great Smoky Mountains National Park

Vegetables

Corn Oysters 1850's

Oysters were very popular in the 1800's, but unless you lived near the ocean, you had to cook pretend oysters. This is a mock oyster dish made from corn.

1 egg, beaten	Milk
½ cup flour	Butter, salt, pepper
6 ears grated fresh sweet corn	

Combine corn, egg, flour, and spices. Add enough milk to make a batter as thick as for pancakes, and stir well. Melt a tablespoon of butter in an iron skillet and drop a spoonful of batter at a time into the hot fat. Cook until brown, then flip and brown the other side. Serves 6.

Photo courtesy Great Smoky Mtns. National Park

Riding a pig in the Smoky Mtns. of Tennessee

Hopping John

1 cup cooked rice	Sausage or ham
1 cup black eyed peas	Salt and pepper

Soak dried peas overnight in water. Drain and cover with fresh water. Cook with a piece of ham or lean sausage until tender and there's not much water left in the pan (about 2 hrs. at a simmer). Add the rice and season with salt and pepper to taste, then toss. Garnish with a mixture of chopped fresh tomatoes, finely chopped onions, and parsley.

VEGETABLES

Photo courtesy Nebraska State Historical Society

The Shores Family, 1887

POTATO SNOW, 1894

"Pare some potatoes, and boil them well, but not so as to be watery. Drain them, and mash and season them well. Press them through a wire sieve into the dish in which they are to be served, salting them before sending them to the table."[30]

How to Find a Lost Object

- *The person who lost the object spits into his right hand and hits the spit spot with the left forefinger. The spittle will spatter in the direction of the lost object.*
- *If you lose something, ask a daddy longlegs spider where it is. He'll lift one of his legs and point in the direction of the lost object.*

FRUIT

Pioneers and farmers ate whatever fruit they could raise or find in the wild. They canned, pickled, dried, and jammed it so they could make it last into the long winter months. After 1870, railcars transported fruit from Florida and South America, but even then, oranges, bananas, and pineapples were too expensive to buy unless there was a special occasion. Berry picking was a favorite job of youngsters, for the chore also included romping, munching, and dozing in the sun.

Photo courtesy Great Smoky Mountains National Park

STRAWBERRY FRUIT LEATHER

On a dry day, puree a pint of strawberries in the blender. Throw in a little sugar and blend well. Spread fruit as thinly as possible onto an oiled cookie sheet. Before you go to bed, put the cookie sheet in a 200° oven, turn off the heat and crack the oven door. In the morning, lift up the fruit and let it continue to dry on a wire cookie rack. When the leather is dry, put it on a piece of plastic wrap and roll it up. You can make leather from most any fruit, though some like peaches and apples will need to be cooked down first.

FRUIT

CITY COURTIN'

Let's say, it's 1850, and you're a young man and you like a girl but you're too shy to tell her directly (that would be impolite, anyway.) So you ask one of your friends to deliver a private message to her using flowers that have certain meanings. These bouquets are called Tussie Mussies. You might send her a white azalea that means "first love" with a pink rose-bud that means "young girl." She might send back forget-me-nots meaning "true love," white rosebuds which mean "I'm too young;" or she could send a bouquet of snap dragons, ragweed, and red geraniums. This heart-breaking bouquet means, "No, you're a nuisance, go away!"

TALKING FRUIT BASKET

Flowers of fruits had meanings, too. If you want to send fruit with a message, consider a combination of any of these:

Lemon	*Zesty, faithful*
Orange	*Happy*
Black Raspberry	*Remorse (you're sorry)*
Red Raspberry	*Fulfillment*
Cherry	*Good job*
Grape	*Plenty, prosperity, happy at home*
Peach	*Feminine, healthy*
Blackberry	*Dangerous*
Strawberry	*You are delicious*

COURTIN'

FRONTIER COURTIN'

Frontier courting was a bit different than city courting. A young man who liked a young woman would send her a note by a friend, called a "compliment." It might say:

Dear Miss Gray,
May I have the plea-
sure of your company at the
pie supper on Sunday night?
Very respectfully yours,
John Peters

Then he would fold the note and write on the outside:

Miss Mary Gray, at home

Next, he would fold a corner of the note down and have his friend deliver the letter. The friend would wait for the young lady's response and deliver her answer to his friend straight away. If she said "yes," on the night of the date, he'd pick her up in his buggy (along with other adult chaperones, of course.) Often, she said "no" because she had no shoes or suitable clothes to wear.[4]

Photo courtesy of Ronnie Myers

19th Century Beauty Tips
- *If you want to be pretty, eat cornfield peas or a hundred chicken gizzards.*
- *To prevent ugliness, don't drink coffee or let the moon shine on your uncovered face.*

FRUIT

FRUIT SALAD

Cut a fresh cantaloupe in half, scoop out seeds and save to make the necklace below. Using a melon baller or a spoon, take the insides out of the cantaloupe and put in a bowl. Add and mix together whatever fresh fruit you have on hand. Strawberries, blueberries, and bananas taste great. Serve fruit in cantaloupe bowls.

PINEAPPLE ICE

This is a delicious and easy treat that combines pioneer simplicity with modern equipment.

Freeze a can of crushed pineapple. Thaw slightly by letting it sit out at room temperature for 30 minutes or set the can in a pan of warm water for 5 minutes. Open the can and put contents into a food processor fitted with a steel blade or a blender. Whirl the pineapple until it turns white. Serve at once. Garnish with a fresh strawberry and a couple green mint leaves.

Job's Tear's Necklace

Job's Tears are the beautiful seeds of a tropical grass called Coix. They are a hard, shiny, grey seed often seen in rosaries. You can make lovely necklaces by stringing Job's Tears alternating with lots of clean, dry melon seeds. String ten or more melon seeds together for the best effect. The seeds are quite difficult to buy, so why don't you grow some? They need a long growing season, but they're not fussy. Seeds are available from:

J.L. Hudson, Seedsman
Star Route 2, Box 337
La Honda, Califrnia 94020
Send $1.00 for a catalog

DESSERT

These desserts are simple, made from ingredients most of us have on hand. Only in the homes of the wealthy city-dwellers would you find fancy desserts in the 1800's. Sugar was a luxury. It was light brown, compressed into cone shapes and wrapped in paper. If you wanted a cake, you had to scrape the sugar from the cone, collect the eggs from the chickens, milk the cows, churn the butter, and feed the fire in the cookstove. That's why kids danced for joy when someone gave them a cookie. They didn't get many.

Have an adult with you as you cook these desserts. Resist the temptation to taste uncooked cookie dough and cake batter because they contain raw eggs which could make you sick. And remember, eat your cookies while they're warm!

Photo courtesy of NDIRS-North Dakota State University

The mother in this picture is probably not baking cookies today, she's busy tending her young children (she had eight), the animals and kitchen garden. Her sod house looks dark, damp, and hard to keep clean. But her land is her own and maybe one day she and her husband will build a wood house with timber brought from the East to their North Dakota territory by railcar.

DESSERT

NUTTY SNOWBALL COOKIES

This is an eggless cookie dough you can sample before baking. Even kids who think they hate nuts love these cookies.

1 stick butter, softened	1 tsp. vanilla
3 Tbs. sugar	1 cup flour
1 cup walnuts or pecans	Powdered sugar

Grind nuts in food processor and set aside. Combine butter, sugar, and vanilla and beat until fluffy. With a spoon, stir in flour and nuts. Roll the dough into small balls, and put on a greased cookie sheet. Bake at 300° for 20 minutes or until LIGHTLY browned.

Put a cup of powdered sugar in a bowl, and roll warm cookies in it until coated. Set cookies on a plate to cool. They freeze great.

TEA CAKES, 1855

1 stick butter, softened	1 tsp. vanilla
1 cup sugar	2 cups flour
1 egg	½ cup whole milk
1 tsp. baking powder	

Combine butter and sugar, and beat until fluffy. Add egg, vanilla, and baking powder and beat until well blended. Beat in flour, and then milk until the mixture is smooth. Butter a baking sheet and space evenly 6 heaping tablespoons of batter. Spread out each portion of dough into a circle the diameter of your hand. Top with sugar or colored sprinkles. Bake at 350° 15 minutes or until lightly browned.

DESSERT

Photo courtesy NDIRS-NDSU, Fargo, N.D.

SLICE AND BAKE SUGAR COOKIES

1 stick butter	1 tsp. baking powder
1 cup sugar	2 cups flour
1 egg	1 tsp. vanilla

Soften butter, then cream with sugar. Add egg, vanilla, and baking powder, and beat some more. Add flour until you have a stiff dough. Roll the dough up in waxed paper and chill until firm. Preheat oven to 350° then butter your cookie sheet. Slice as many cookies as you want to bake (about ¼ inch thick.) Decorate with sprinkles or leave plain. Bake 10 minutes or until lightly browned.

FACE COOKIES

Slice off circles of chilled sugar cookie dough and place on a buttered cookie sheet. Mix some of the dough with food coloring and add eyes, eyebrows, mouth, nose, ears, hair to your cookie. See what kind of wild expressions you can create. To make brown faces and hair, add a little cocoa powder or melted chocolate chips to some of the cookie dough and mix well, then chill. Bake the faces like the sugar cookies above.

SHOES

Photo courtesy Great Smoky Mountains National Park

Shoes?

Most rural early American children didn't wear them. Shoe-makers were uncommon on the frontier, and who had money to cover 24 growing feet anyway? Kids saved shoes from getting worn out by wearing them only in Winter and on special occasions.

In this photo, a woman from the rugged Smoky Mountains of East Tennessee stands next to her cabin with 6 of her 12 children. The photographer supplied them with dresses and dolls, but their bare feet poke through, reminding us of the scarcity of the most simple things in the lives of the pioneers who settled our country.

DESSERT

THUMBPRINT COOKIES

Make a recipe of sugar cookies and chill the dough for 30 minutes. Roll the chilled dough into 1 inch balls and place on a greased cookie sheet. Punch your thumb into each cookie and fill the space with a little bit of raspberry jam. If you add too much jam, it will bubble over onto the cookie sheet and burn. Bake at 350° for 15 minutes or until lightly browned.

Photo courtesy Denver Public Library

1887 Menu Suggestion for a Monday

Breakfast: *Baked apples, hominy, broiled white fish, ham omelet, potatoes with cream, parker house rolls, crullers, toast, coffee.*

Lunch: *Cold roast turkey, Boston oyster pie, celery salad, baked sweet potatoes, rusks, fruit cake, sliced oranges, tea.*

Dinner: *Macaroni soup, boiled leg of mutton with caper sauce, potatoes a la Delmonico, steamed cabbage, cheese fondue, pickles, lemon pudding, jelly kisses, raisins, nuts, fruit, coffee.*[30]

DESSERT

APPLE UPSIDE DOWN CAKE

Topping:

2 Tbs. butter   ½ cup brown sugar
5 tart apples   Cinnamon

Peel and slice apples into ½ inch wedges. Melt butter in a 10-inch iron skillet. Throw in the apples and cook about 5 minutes. Add sugar and stir until it melts. Spread mixture evenly in pan, then sprinkle with cinnamon.

Cake:

1 stick butter   1½ cup flour
½ cup brown sugar   1 tsp. baking powder
½ cup white sugar   1 tsp. cinnamon
2 eggs   1 tsp. vanilla
3 tart apples, diced

Beat softened butter with sugars until fluffy. Add eggs and vanilla and beat some more. Now beat in baking powder and cinnamon. Next add flour and beat until combined. Use a spoon to stir in the apples. The batter will be thick. Spread it on top on the apple mixture in the skillet and bake in a preheated 350° oven for 45 minutes or until lightly browned and a cake baker says it's done.

Let cake cool about 10 minutes, then have a grown-up invert the skillet onto a large plate. Serve warm. Whipped cream? Yes!

DESSERT

REALLY EASY
GINGERBREAD APPLE UPSIDE DOWN CAKE

We make this on camping trips in a cast iron dutch oven. You can even prepare this in a zip lock bag! Just add the ingredients and boil the bag until the cake's done.

1 box gingerbread mix (the "add only water" kind)
1 can apple pie filling

Butter the bottom of a 10 inch cast iron skillet or a 9 inch baking dish. Cover the bottom of the pan with the apple pie filling. Mix up the gingerbread according to package directions and spread evenly on top of the apples. Cover the top with foil and bake at 350° until cake springs back when you touch it, about 25 minutes. To serve, spoon the cake onto plates and cover with apples.

*If using a dutch oven, put your pan on a small bed of coals and put about 12 charcoal sized coals on the lid. Bake until you smell the apples and it looks done.

Photo by Wayne Erbsen

51

SCHOOL

H ow would you like to walk five miles to and from school each day? If you lived in rural America in 1850, that's what you would have done. That is, after you milked the cows and fed the chickens and pigs. In fact, you'd only have gone to school four months a year when you weren't needed for farming. Rural children attended one room schools with grades 1-8 together. City children were grouped according to age or ability in grades.

Communities thought it was the job of the school to teach children the 3 R's (Reading, Writing, Arithmetic), and correct moral behavior as well. Discipline was strict, especially for older boys who could hunt, plow, rope bulls...and didn't want to be told what to do by a teacher only one year older than they were!

Few children could afford books, so they carried only a slate, chalk, and tin lunch pail to school. Lunch would have been leftover breakfast: biscuit or cornbread, ham, dried fruit, maybe a potato. Teachers were poorly paid and boarded with the families whose children they taught. Just think of it...at the end of the day, your teacher goes home with you. No excuses like "the chickens ate my homework" for you!

Photo courtesy Library of Congress

DESSERT

Photo courtesy of North Dakota Institute for Regional Studies, NDSU

These North Dakota children are playing a game during school recess. Can you guess what game it is?

PERSIMMON PUDDING

I know, this recipe sounds disgusting. But it's really good, a moist cake that tastes like date bars. Use the old-timey little persimmons that grow in the mountains. They ripen and fall from the trees in late summer. You know they're ready if they're purple, wrinkled, and smushy sweet inside. You know they're not ripe if your cheek sticks to your tongue from puckering! Use chopped dates as a substitute if you don't have a persimmon tree.

1 cup thick persimmon pulp, seeds strained out
1 egg   ¾ cup sugar
1 cup milk   1 tsp. vanilla
1 cup flour   ½ tsp. baking soda
Pinch salt   Pinch allspice or ginger
2 Tbs. melted butter

Combine pulp, sugar, butter, and egg and beat well. Add salt, soda, spice, and vanilla and beat until blended. Blend in milk and flour until smooth. Pour into a large buttered baking dish and bake at 300° for 30 minutes or until lightly browned. Cut into small squares and top with fresh whipped cream.

DESSERT

Photo courtesy N.C. Archives and History

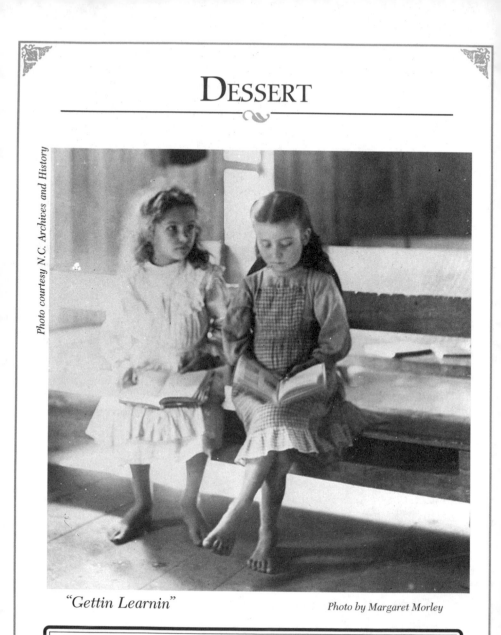

"Gettin Learnin"

Photo by Margaret Morley

You'll Get a Whippin' if...

- *Your back itches*
- *You wear two hats, one atop the other*
- *You sing in bed*
- *You dream of muddy water*
- *A girl dreams of holes in her stockings*

DESSERT

CHERRY, BERRY, OR APPLE PIE

2 recipes for pie pastry   Sugar
Fresh fruit   Corn starch

Roll out a pie crust and put it in the bottom of the pie pan. You'll need 6 large apples or at least 2 cups berries. Slice apples, but leave cherries or berries whole. Put the fruit in a bowl and add ¼ cup sugar. (If using sour cherries or blackberries, add ¾ cup sugar.) Toss fruit, sugar, and about 2 Tbs. corn starch (3 Tbs. for black-berries) until blended. Pour into pie pan, piled high in the middle. Put on your top crust, seal, and slice 3 vent holes in to top. Place on a cookie sheet and bake in a 350° oven for 45 minutes or until it bubbles over the vent holes. Cover lightly with foil after 30 min-utes to prevent over-browning.

PIE PASTRY

A good pie crust is a work of art. Not just any-one can make one, but I'll bet you can! Remem-ber, even if your pastry falls apart so much that you can't use it for a pie, you can cut it in strips and sprinkle cinnamon sugar on it before baking just like cookies.

For one large crust (bottom or top):

        1 cup all purpose flour
        1/3 cup butter or solid vegetable shortening
        ½ tsp. salt
        ¼ cup ice water

Mix the salt in with the flour then rub the butter into it until the butter lumps are smaller than peas. This is the tricky part...add the water and stir until the dough barely holds together. If you add too much water, you'll have a tough dough. Form the dough into a ball and knead on a floured board a few times until it holds together. Don't handle the dough too much or your warm little hands will melt the fat, and you won't have a flaky crust. Now roll the dough out on a floured board into the shape you want it. You'll have to do some pie research to learn how to shape the edges. Bake sales and bakeries are good places to do research!

DESSERT

APPLE TURNOVERS

Make a recipe for pie pastry and roll it out into a square shape. Cut your big square into 4 smaller squares. Fold your pastry so it makes a triangle shape. Pile ¼ of the apple filling in the center of the bottom triangle, then pinch the ends of the pastry closed. Fold a little piece of the bottom crust over the top crust and pinch closed again with a fork. The filling will leak out if you don't do all this folding and pinching. Bake on a cookie sheet lined with foil at 350° for 25 minutes or until browned.

Filling: Peel and slice thinly 5 large apples. (Any kind of apple except Red Delicious will make a good pie.) Mix in one teaspoon cinnamon, ½ cup sugar, and 2 level Tablespoons flour.

Moist and Chewy Mud Pies

Gather as many large, whole leaves as you have guests. Put a scoop of rich, dark mud on top of each leaf. Stir in chopped pine cones if you like that sort of thing. Bake in the hot sun until just dried around the edges but still moist in the middle. Sprinkle fresh dirt on top and serve at once. These taste especially good if you "eat" them on the bank of a creek with your bare feet in the water.

DESSERT

FUDGE SNOW TAFFY

This is actually a recipe for Hot Fudge Sauce to be poured over ice cream. The longer you cook it, the chewier it gets, so pour it over packed snow for a treat you'll never forget. **Warning:** *If you have braces or fillings, cook taffy 2 minutes less than suggested below. Have an adult do the boiling and pouring.*

1½ oz. baking chocolate	¼ cup boiling water
1 Tbs. butter	1 cup sugar
2 Tbs. light corn syrup	1 tsp. vanilla extract

Melt the chocolate and butter over very, very low heat. Add everything else except vanilla, and slowly bring to a boil. Boil the mixture for 5-8 minutes. Pour cold water in a teacup and add ice. Your taffy is ready if chocolate drizzled into ice water stiffens and holds it's shape. When done, take the pan off the stove and stir in vanilla. Let it cool slightly before drizzling the chocolate over packed snow. No snow? Well then just pour it on vanilla ice cream!

Snow Candles

All you need for this simple project is candle wax, wicking, and a crock pot.

Fill a wide mouth quart jar with wax pieces. Put the jar into a crockpot ¼ filled with warm water. Cover and heat until wax melts. Now put your snow clothes on and pack a pile of snow. Dig a hole out in the snow the size you want your candle to be. Have an adult pour the melted wax into the hole and let it harden slightly on the outside. Tie a piece of wick the length of your candle onto a pencil. Set the pencil on top of the candle so the wick goes down into the wax. When the candle is hardened, pick it out of the snow and put it on a small plate before lighting.

DESSERT

SUGAR PLUMS

Sugar plums were actually candied figs or dried plums stuffed with almonds or pecans. For a sugar plum tree, poke a nut into dried fruit, wrap with foil, and hang on your holiday tree with colored ribbon. The recipe below requires an adult to cook the syrup.

Have an adult make a syrup by boiling one cup sugar and ½ cup hot water to the hard crack stage (300°). It's ready when a spoonful of syrup dropped in cold water creates brittle threads. Stuff dried fruit (apricots, dates, figs) with an almond and pierce with a bamboo skewer, one at a time. Older kids can dip the fruit into the syrup and let it dry on waxed paper. You can dip orange sections that have been allowed to dry for 8 hours, too. Unless you live in the desert, you'll need to eat your sugar plums the same day you make them. Leave fruit unglazed for hanging on your holiday tree.

Pioneer Holiday Gifts

If you were the child of a pioneer family, you would be thrilled if you got this in your stocking on Christmas morning: An orange, peppermint stick, penny, and maybe a cookie.

DESSERT

POPCORN BALLS

An adult will need to do the syrup cooking, but you can form the mixture into balls once the mixture is cool enough to handle.

1 quart popped corn	1 Tbs. butter
1 cup brown sugar	2 Tbs. light corn syrup
4 Tbs. water	Pinch salt

Combine the sugar, corn syrup, water, and butter. Stir until sugar is mostly dissolved. Cover, and lightly boil for 3 minutes. Uncover, and simmer 5 more minutes. Drop a little in cold water, if you can get it to hold together into a soft ball; then it's cooked enough. Take the syrup off the stove, and add the salt. Put the popcorn in a LARGE bowl and pour the syrup over it, tossing with a spoon. Dump the coated popcorn onto waxed paper and when it's cool enough to handle, the kids can butter their hands and form the popcorn balls.

Photo by Gideon Laney courtesy of David Anderson

Reptile Lore

- *If you hold lizard eggs in your hands, you'll break plates.*
- *Rub your hands with a black snake's shedded skin, and you won't break plates.*

CHORES

I n 1914, a law was passed making child labor illegal. Children under the age of 14 were no longer allowed to work in businesses or commercial fields in this country. Before that time, children worked long hours in factories and vegetable fields for very little pay because their families needed the extra money just to survive.

Photo Courtesy Library of Congress

The child in this photo is working in the shrimp and oyster industry. He is standing in front of a giant pile of sharp oyster shells wearing no shoes. A man named Lewis Hine took this picture in 1911. His famous photographs of child labor in America helped to pass the law prohibiting young children from working in unhealthy environments like this.

CHORES

I f you were a child of a settler family, you worked long hours every day, too. But at least you were with your family, and not in a factory or field. Many pioneer families chose to resettle so far from home to escape the desperate working conditions of the cities where they lived.

There was so much work to be done on the frontier that pioneers had to combine work with play in the form of work parties. There were bean stringin's, taffy pulls, sugarin-off parties (boiling down maple sap to make syrup), and quilting bees. Teens looked forward to corn shuckin' parties. If a boy found a red ear of corn, he could kiss any girl in the room!

Photo courtesy Great Smoky Mtns. National Park

Hauling water from the spring

Household Toys From an 1880 Catalog

Chores of the Pioneer Child

Water hauling, fire tending, feeding the chickens, collecting eggs, milking the cow, churning butter, tending the kitchen garden, canning vegetables, candle dipping, quilting, sewing, mending, hunting, fishing.

FOLK REMEDIES

Back before germs were discovered in the 1880's, people weren't sure how diseases were spread from one person to the next. And they didn't know how to cure them either. Sometimes folks made up crazy ways to prevent getting sick, called superstitions. Although we know much about diseases today, lots of superstitions have been passed down from generation to generation, still surfacing in the play of children. You all know the rhyme, "Step on a crack, break your mother's back." Here are some old-timey folk remedies that were once thought to cure diseases or even prevent slobbering!

Photo courtesy Great Smoky Mtns. National Park

TO CURE CHICKEN POX
• Get under the chicken roost and scare the chickens away.
• Let a chicken fly over the victim's head before breakfast.
• Go to a hog barn and lie down. Roll over three times, then get up, walk backwards thirty three steps, and the chicken pox will be cured.

FOLK REMEDIES

TO PREVENT SLOBBERING
Carry a thimbleful of water to a month old baby without spilling a drop.

TO PREVENT CROSS-EYES
Don't let a baby look into a mirror.

TREATMENT FOR FRECKLES (1885)
"Freckles indicate a defective digestion, caused by fatty matter beneath the skin. Squeeze ½ lemon into a goblet of water and put on the face morning and night. But don't use too much or you'll get wrinkles."[20]

TO STOP HICCOUGHS

- Think of a fox with no tail.
- Eat Damson plum jam.
- Take nine swallows of water and walk backward nine steps.
- Look real hard into the middle of a glass.
- Hold your breath and count to 50 backwards.
- Think of your lover; if he loves you the hiccoughs will go away.

19th Century Childhood Diseases

Polio, Measles, Mumps, Diptheria, Whooping Cough, Chicken Pox, Smallpox, Typhoid Fever, Tuberculosis, Cholera, Malaria, and Scarlet Fever

FRONTIER HYGIENE

You may be surprised to know that American pioneers took a bath only on Saturday night, and washed their hair maybe once a month, if that. But they were clean compared to how folks lived in the 1700's. Colonial Americans almost never took baths. They thought that cleaning the oil off your skin made you vulnerable to illness. If you were a traveling man spending the night in a tavern, you'd sleep on a bed whose linens were washed twice a year. And because there were more boarders than beds, you'd sleep next to at least two other grimy, smelly men you didn't even know!

HAIR

Each family had one comb and brush that everyone shared. A very special gift from a husband or fiance might have been a brush, or a mirror purchased at the general store with precious long-saved earnings.

Advice on shampooing ranged from never to weekly. Some women brushed oil into their hair instead of washing it, but most washed their hair at least once a month with homemade soap.

Photo courtesy Mars Hill College, N.C.

A father gives his boys summer haircuts on the front porch of his mountain cabin.

Frontier Hygiene

Photo courtesy Denver Public Library

Chewing Gum

Chewing gum was called "wax" in the South, and it was scarce. Instead of chewing the gum a while and spitting it out, it was passed around from child to child FOR DAYS!!![4]

Tooth Brushing

The pioneer toothbrush was a twig chewed on the end. For toothpaste, you could dip your twig in salt and brush; or maybe a mixture of charcoal, soap, and chalk was more to your liking.

Drinking Water

Whether at home or in a public building like the mercantile, there was one bucket of water with a dipper-gourd that all thirsty drinkers would share. Then you'd dry your face and hands on one dirty community towel. This is how Typhoid (called slow fever) and many other diseases were passed around.

MORE RECIPES

More Recipes

MORE RECIPES

BIBLIOGRAPHY

BOOKS

1. Aunt Callie and Others, *Our Boys Chatterbox*, 1884
2. Beard, D.C., *The American Boys Handy Book*, 1890
3. Beard, Lina & Adelia *The American Girls Handy Book*, 1887
4. Bell, Marianne, *Frontier Family Life*, 1998
5. Boatright, Hudson, & Maxwell, *Texas Folk & Folklore*, 1954
6. Brown, Frank C., *North Carolina Folklore*, 1996
7. Child, Lydia Maria, *The American Frugal Housewife*, 1833
8. Child, Lydia Maria, *The Girl's Own Book*, 1834
9. *Country Holidays*, M.A. Donohue & Co., Chicago, 1888
10. Dale, Edward Everett, *Frontier Ways*, 1959
11. Fisher, Abby, *What Mrs. Fisher Knows About Old Southern Cooking*, 1881, Reprint, Applewood Books
12. Freedman, Russell, *Children of the Wild West*, 1983
13. Grunfeld, Frederic V., *Games of the World*, UNICEF, 1982
14. Hermence, Belinda, *My Folks Don't Want Me to Talk about Slavery*, 1998
15. Hermence, Belinda, *We Lived in a Little Cabin in the Yard*, 1998
16. Hermence, Belinda, *Before Freedom When I Just Can Remember*, 1998 John Blair Pub., 1406 Plaza Dr., Winston-Salem, N.C. 27103
17. Hiner, Ray and Hawes, Joseph, *Growing Up in America: Children in Historical Perspective*, 1985
18. Marcy, Randolph, *The Prairie Traveler, 1859*, Reprint Applewood Books, 1993
19. Mintz, Steven and Kellgg, Susan, *Domestic Revolutions: A Social History of American Family Life*, 1988
20. *Practical Housekeeping*, Buckeye Publishing, 1885
21. *Rainbow Stories*, McLoughlin Bros., N.Y., 1898
22. Randolph, Mary, *The Virginia Housewife*, 1824, Reprint Dover Books
23. Randolph, Vance, *Ozark Superstitions*, 1946
24. *The New Home Cookbook*, by "A Ladies' Club", 1925
25. *The Cook's Own Book* by a Boston Housekeeper, 1832, Reprint Rare Book Publishers
26. Thomas, Daniel and Lucy, *Kentucky Superstitions*, 1920
27. *Williamsburg Art of Cookery*, Colonial Williamsburg, 1938
28. Wilson, Charles, *Backwoods America*, 1934
29. Winslow, Marjorie, *Mud Pies and Other Recipies: A Cookbook for Dolls*, 1961
30. Ziemann, Hugo and Gillette, Mrs. F.L. *The Whitehouse Cookbook*, 1894

CREDITS

THANKS!

To taste testers, Wayne, Annie, Wes, and Rita Erbsen, Justin Hallman, and Sybil Hogan. Recipe and research contributors included Nancy Swell, Richard Renfro, Marti Otto, Laura Wright. Computer support, Leon Swell. Editing, Lori Erbsen, Janet Swell, Bonnie Neustein, and Beverly Teeman. Thanks to Steve Millard for graphic and cover design.

Native Ground Music

BOOKS OF SONGS & LORE

Backpocket Bluegrass Songbook
Backpocket Old-Time Songbook
Cowboy Songs, Jokes, Lingo 'n Lore
Front Porch Songs, Jokes & Stories
Log Cabin Pioneers
Old-Time Gospel Songbook
Outlaw Ballads, Legends & Lore
Railroad Fever
Rousing Songs & True Tales
  of the Civil War
Singing Rails

INSTRUCTION BOOKS

5-String Banjo for the
  Complete Ignoramus!
Bluegrass Banjo Simplified!!
Starting Bluegrass Banjo
  From Scratch
Painless Guide to the Guitar
Painless Mandolin Melodies
Southern Mountain Banjo
Southern Mountain Fiddle
Southern Mountain Mandolin
Southern Mountain Dulcimer

RECORDINGS

An Old-Fashioned Wingding
Authentic Outlaw Ballads
Ballads & Songs of the
  Civil War
Bullfrogs on Your Mind
Cold Frosty Morning
Cowboy Songs of the
  Wild Frontier
Front Porch Favorites
Log Cabin Songs
Love Songs of the Civil War
The Home Front
Old-Time Gospel Favorites
Old-Time Gospel Instrumentals
Raccoon and a Possum
Sing it Yourself!
Songs of the Santa Fe Trail
Southern Mountain Classics
Southern Soldier Boy
The Home Front
Waterdance

Three other great Native Ground books by Barbara Swell:
- **LOG CABIN COOKING**
- **TAKE TWO AND BUTTER 'EM WHILE THEY'RE HOT!**
- **SECRETS OF THE OLD TIMEY COOKS**

Write or call for a FREE Catalog
NATIVE GROUND MUSIC
109 Bell Road
Asheville, NC 28805-1521

800-752-2656
EMAIL:
banjo@nativeground.com
WEB SITE:
www.nativeground.com

71

Recipe Index